SHERLOCK HOLMES IN

THE ADVENTURE

OF THE

SPECKLED BAND

by Sir Arthur Conan Doyle

Retold by Helen Johnson

Illustrated by Peter Wilks

Series Editors: Steve Barlow and Steve Skidmore

Published by Heinemann Educational Publishers
Halley Court, Jordan Hill, Oxford OX2 8EJ
A division of Reed Educational and Professional Publishing Ltd

OXFORD   MELBOURNE   AUCKLAND
JOHANNESBURG   BLANTYRE   GABORONE
IBADAN   PORTSMOUTH NH (USA)   CHICAGO

First published 2000
2004   2003   2002 2001   2000
10 9   8   7   6   5   4   3   2   1
ISBN 0 435 21388 1

Illustrations by Peter Wilks
Cover design by Shireen Nathoo Design
Cover artwork by Mark Oldroyd
Designed by Artistix, Thame, Oxon
Printed and bound in Great Britain by Athenaeum Press Ltd

Tel: 01865 888058 www.heinemann.co.uk

Contents

Characters

Sherlock Holmes is a great detective. He can solve any crime.

Dr Watson is Holmes' friend and helper.

Helen Stoner is
a rich young lady.
She thinks that
someone is trying
to kill her.

Julia Stoner was
Helen's sister.
She was killed
two years ago.

Dr Roylott is
Helen and
Julia's stepfather.

Introduction

Sherlock Holmes is the greatest detective that ever lived. He sees clues that other people miss. His mind is like a machine. He can solve any crime.

Take the case of the Speckled Band. Julia Stoner died alone in her bed. Her door was locked. The windows were barred. Nobody could get into that room. Yet somebody had killed her. And now they were trying to kill her sister. Holmes had to find out who…

CHAPTER 1

It was April 1883. I woke up to find Sherlock Holmes standing by my bed.

'Get up, Watson!' he said. 'We have a visitor.'

I looked at my watch. It was very early.

'Come on!' said Holmes. 'We have a case to solve.'

I jumped out of bed and dressed quickly.

Holmes was already downstairs. A woman was sitting in the chair by the fire. She was dressed all in black.

Her face was pale. The fire was lit but she was shivering.

Holmes pointed to me. 'This is Dr Watson,' he said. 'And I am Sherlock Holmes. How can we help you?'

The woman looked at us. 'My name is Helen Stoner. I … ' A door slammed outside and she jumped. Her eyes were wide with fear.

Holmes walked over to the fireplace.

'I see you have come a long way this morning, Miss Stoner,' he said.

'Why, yes!' she said. 'All the way from Surrey. How on earth did you know?'

Holmes smiled. 'It was easy. I saw the train ticket inside your glove. And there is fresh mud on your skirt.'

'I started out before six o'clock this morning,' said Miss Stoner. 'I was too frightened to sleep. Mr Holmes, please say you will help me. You are the only person who can.'

Holmes raised an eyebrow. 'Please tell me why you have come, Miss Stoner.'

The woman played with the gloves in her hand. 'Last night while I was in my room I heard a whistle.'

Holmes stopped walking around the room and frowned. 'A whistle, you say?'

Miss Stoner nodded. 'I was sleeping in my sister's room. She died in that very same room two weeks before her wedding. And just before she died she heard the same sound – a whistle.'

I wondered how a whistle could kill anybody.

'When was this?' asked Holmes. 'When did your sister die?'

Miss Stoner stared down at her hands. 'Two years ago,' she said.

'Two years! Why have you waited all this time before coming to see me?'

'Because I was not afraid for my life before,' Miss Stoner replied.

CHAPTER 2

Miss Stoner told us about herself. She and her twin sister Julia were born in India. Their father died and their mother married Dr Roylott.

'Dr Roylott had no money but my mother was rich. We came to England and moved into the Manor House at Stoke Moran. At first we were happy. But then my mother died. My sister and I were left alone. My stepfather is a hard man. He made us work in the house. We rarely went out.'

'Don't you have any visitors?' asked
Holmes.

Miss Stoner shook her head.
'Dr Roylott has no friends. Nobody ever
comes to the house. They are too scared of
him and his animals,' she said.

'What animals are these?' asked Holmes.

'A cheetah and a baboon. My
stepfather loves Indian animals. He lets
them go free in the grounds.'

Holmes closed his eyes briefly. 'Do go
on, Miss Stoner.'

'We never visited anyone except
my aunt,' said Miss Stoner. 'It was there that
my sister Julia met the man she was to
marry. But since Julia died I have been on
my own.'

She began to cry.

Holmes patted her arm. 'Tell me about the night your sister died.'

Helen Stoner took a deep breath. 'I couldn't sleep that night. The wind was blowing hard and it was raining. Then I heard a scream. I jumped out of bed. As I ran to my sister's room I thought I heard a whistle. Then there was a loud bang. It was as if somebody had dropped a heavy pan or tea tray.'

Miss Stoner shook again as she remembered her sister's death.

'Julia's door was open. She was standing in the doorway. Her face was as white as paper. She fell to the floor, crying in pain.

'When she saw me she cried out, "Oh, my God, Helen! It was the band! The speckled band!"'

CHAPTER 3

'The speckled band?' repeated Holmes.
He tapped his lip. 'What did your sister
mean by this?'

'I don't know.' She shook her head.

'Was the whistle outside?' Holmes asked.

'I'm not sure. The storm was very loud.
Dr Roylott came running from his room to
save Julia. But it was no good.'

Holmes stared into the fire. 'You say
your sister was alone. Could somebody have
entered her room without you seeing?'

'No. We always locked our doors at night because of the animals. And the windows are barred.'

Holmes nodded. 'But why were you sleeping in your sister's room last night?'

'A few weeks ago an old friend asked me to marry him. My stepfather agreed to the marriage. He said we could live at Stoke Moran after the wedding. He even offered to paint my room. So I am sleeping in my sister's room while the painters are there.'

Holmes lifted his head sharply.

'Miss Stoner, we will come to Stoke Moran at once.'

When Miss Stoner had gone, Holmes turned to me and said. 'Dr Roylott has a reason to kill her. The family money belongs to the girls. He will lose his fortune if either of them marries. But he was in his room when Julia Stoner died.'

Suddenly the door burst open. A large man was standing in the doorway. He wore a black top hat and coat. He held a whip in one hand. His face was red with sunburn.

'Which of you is Holmes?' he shouted.

'I am,' said Holmes.

The man was shaking with rage. 'I've heard of your busy-bodying!' he shouted. 'I'm Doctor Grimesby Roylott of Stoke Moran. I'm warning you to keep your nose out of my affairs!'

He grabbed the poker from the fireplace and bent it into a curve.

'Let that be a warning to you,' he boomed. Then he threw down the poker and stormed out.

'Well, well!' laughed Holmes. 'What a nice man! I think we have just met Miss Stoner's stepfather.' Holmes bent the poker until it was straight again. 'And now, Watson, we must go to Stoke Moran before Dr Roylott gets there.'

CHAPTER 4

Stoke Moran was a big old house. We met Miss Stoner outside.

'The bedrooms are here on the ground floor,' said Miss Stoner. 'That is the window to my room. This middle one was my sister's room. The one at the far end is my stepfather's.'

Holmes went over to the middle window. He looked at it with his lens. Then he asked Miss Stoner to go inside and close the shutters.

The metal shutter bars fell with a loud clang.

'This could be the noise Miss Stoner heard,' Holmes said to me. Then he tried to force the shutters open. He was very strong, but he could not open the shutters at all.

We went inside. The three bedrooms led off one long corridor. Holmes joined Miss Stoner in her sister's old room. He began to inspect the walls and floor.

It was a small room. It had a low ceiling and a big fireplace. There was a bed in one corner and a small chest of drawers in another. Holmes looked around the room. He saw the long bell-rope which hung over the bed. The end was resting on the pillow.

'That looks new,' he said.

'Yes. My stepfather put it in a couple of years ago. My sister never used it. If we wanted anything, we got it ourselves.'

Holmes nodded. Then he got down on his hands and knees. Miss Stoner looked surprised, but I was used to Holmes's ways. We watched as he crawled over the boards. He tapped them and examined the cracks with his lens. Then he did the same with the walls. Finally, he gave the bell-rope a sharp tug.

'As I thought – this bell-rope is a dummy,' he said.

'You mean it doesn't work?' I asked.

'Exactly. The rope should be tied to a bell. When the rope is pulled, the bell should ring.

'This rope is not tied to a bell at all. Look – you can see it is just tied to a hook above this vent.'

The bell-rope was hanging over a small opening in the wall above the bed.

'That's odd too,' said Holmes. 'Why have an air vent which leads into another room? It would be better to have fresh air from outside. Who sleeps in the next room?' asked Holmes.

'My stepfather,' said Miss Stoner.

We went into Dr Roylott's room.

There was a shelf full of books, a camp bed and a big iron safe. Miss Stoner told us the Doctor kept his papers in the safe. Holmes picked up a saucer which was standing on top of the safe.

He sniffed it.

'Milk! Do you keep a cat?' he asked.

'Only Dr Roylott's cheetah.'

'I don't think a saucer of milk would make much of a meal for such a large animal!' said Holmes. 'And what is this?'

He held up what looked like a dog's lead. It had been coiled to make a loop. Holmes put his finger in the loop and pulled until it was tight. His face became grim.

'We must spend the night in your sister's room, Miss Stoner,' he said. 'I believe there may be great danger.'

CHAPTER 5

Holmes and I went to the local inn to wait until it was dark. Helen Stoner was going to shine a light when Dr Roylott had gone to bed.

'What did you think of the bed, Watson? Did it not strike you as odd?'

'I saw nothing strange about it,' I said.

'That is because you look, but do not see,' said Holmes. 'The bed was stuck to the floor. Now why should that be?'

But before I had time to think, Holmes jumped to his feet. A light was shining from one of the windows in the manor.

'That is our signal. Come, Watson! It is time to go. And bring your gun!'

We ran out into the night. I followed Holmes into Julia Stoner's bedroom. Helen Stoner had left the window open for us.

Holmes put a finger to his lips, to warn me not to make a sound. I sat in the chair and put the gun on the table beside me. I hoped I would not have to use it. Holmes sat on the bed and put a long thin cane beside him. He also set out a box of matches and a candle. Then we waited.

It was a long night. Outside we heard the church bell ring every hour. Suddenly there was a flash of light through the vent and the smell of burning oil. Someone in the next room had lit a lamp. My eyes strained to see.

Then I heard a small noise, like steam escaping from a kettle. Holmes jumped up. He struck a match and started lashing out at the bell-rope with his cane.

Somewhere, I heard a low, clear whistle.

'Do you see it, Watson?' yelled Holmes, thrashing at the rope.

But the flare of the match had half blinded me. I could only see the look of horror on Holmes's face as he hit out again and again. I gripped the handle of the gun and felt my heart pounding. Then there was the most terrible cry. It seemed to come through the vent.

'What on earth…?' I began.

But Holmes was already opening the door. 'Come on, Watson!'

As I turned into the corridor, I saw Holmes knocking at Dr Roylott's door. He went inside. Dr Roylott was sitting on the chair in his dressing gown.

The safe door was wide open. Lying across his lap was the coiled dog's lead. His head was thrown back and his eyes were staring at the ceiling. He was dead. Around his forehead was a strange yellow band with brownish spots.

'The speckled band!' whispered Holmes.

I leaned forward and the band began to move. It raised its head up in the lamplight.

'It's a swamp adder!' said Holmes. 'A deadly snake from India.'

Holmes caught the snake with the noose of the dog's lead. He threw it into the safe and slammed the door. The clang of metal rang round the room.

CHAPTER 6

Holmes told poor Miss Stoner the news. She was shocked and upset. The next morning we put her on the train to her aunt's house. I think she was glad to leave Stoke Moran.

On the way home, Holmes explained, 'A strange case, Watson. I was wrong at first. I thought the loud noise was the shutter bars falling.

'But once I had seen the room, I knew the killer could not have come from outside the house.

'Miss Stoner told us that the Doctor kept Indian animals. When I saw the bell-rope and the vent, I knew a snake was involved. The bed had been fixed to the floor. It could not be moved away from the rope. The snake would crawl down the bell-rope to kill Miss Stoner.'

'But what about the whistle? And the milk? And the dog's lead?' I asked.

'They were used to train the snake,' said Holmes. 'I have read about snakes being trained. Milk is often used as a reward.

'And the lead was used to catch the snake and return it to its hiding place in the safe.

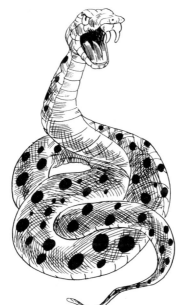

'The noise Miss Stoner heard was the bang of the safe door slamming shut.'

I remembered the look of horror on Holmes's face as he hit the snake with his cane. 'It's a good job you hit it when you did,' I said.

'Yes. I heard its evil hiss as it went down the rope. Of course, once the snake was hit, it turned back. It went back through the vent. There it bit the first thing it saw.' Holmes placed his fingertips together and leaned back in his seat. 'Dr Roylott became a victim of his own evil plans. And I can't say I am sorry.'